From Nightmares to Dreams

Ilene Pauley-Holcombe

FROM NIGHTMARES TO DREAMS

Table of Contents

Dedication

God blessed me with several people along the course of my life to help nurture and guide me. Some of those people did not even share my same beliefs or faith, but followed God's principles and imparted them onto me.

I would like to dedicate this book to almighty God who I recognize as the one who raised me, and I know this divine intervention has taken me *From Nightmares To Dreams*, and beyond. Several women have played a role throughout my journey. The first person was a childhood friend, (Lacey) who acknowledged, supported, encouraged, and advocated for me in the early years of my trauma. This friend's love and support was the foundation of the beginning of me having hope for life.

My Aunt Ella Berry left me a short note one day saying that she was able to see some of what I was going through and could relate.

This statement from my maternal grandmother, Irene Holcombe "That girl gone make something out of herself one day."

These small things were tucked away for safekeeping.

Betty Jones, the advisor to the sorority I joined, had some idea that I needed her special intervention. She provided me with a job of babysitting her toddler son to help me earn money. She also exposed me to positive new experiences.

Another female entered my life (Evelyn) a couple of years prior to my first college degree. This person reintroduced me to Jesus Christ, with hope that this relationship would expound beyond college.

Mary Chames who was from Mobile, both she and her sister Jacqueline Williams worked at Thee Alabama State University. I changed my work study site from the dining hall and transferred to the library. The administrative assistant assigned me to work in the curriculum department where Ms. Chames was the manager. The assistant stated that she felt this was a good choice because Ms. Chames and I were from Mobile. Ms. Chames became like a mother to me and gave me lots of womanly advice. She invited me into her home for holiday meals and into her family. To add, her dear loving sister Dr. Jacqueline Williams always inspired me, and one of the most encouraging thoughts that resonates when I feel like giving up is "As long as there is life, there is hope."

Introduction

From Nightmares to Dreams tells the story of how good God has been to me throughout my life. He has provided protection like I never knew or could have imagined. I guess my true journey started when I was in my pre-teens as I remember seeing the Ten Commandments on TV and decided I wanted to be like Moses. I even found a stick to call my staff that I used to practice throwing on the ground hoping that it had some special powers. I also remember getting books about God from the library and reading some of those stories to one of my grandmother's elderly friends in the neighborhood. I also used to practice preaching after church to my little cousins about what the pastor had said in the sermon that day. Some years later, one of those cousins reminded me, she said "Ilene do you remember telling us that Jesus was coming back?"

At age 13 my life changed tremendously in a way that I would not have imagined. My nightmares turned into reality. It has taken me so long to begin starting this book again. I guess after reading someone else's book that was not too lengthy, I was inspired to just do it. I guess some hesitation has been letting others know just what my life was like. I became inspired to resume writing after attending the Woman Thou Art Loosed Homecoming Conference in Atlanta, GA with some friends, one of whom I call sister. I felt loosed from my life traumas that kept haunting me. Most people seem to always think that everyone's life includes a supportive family and closeness among parents and siblings. Sure, we all know that this is not true however no one seems to think that a person who has experienced those traumas is sitting right in front of them, namely me. I had to realize prior to completing this book, that the trauma associated with my abuse begin among my mother and my maternal siblings and have continued with their children. At a young age I became the primary caregiver to my siblings and this is where the victimization begins. Within the page of the book, I am outlining the details of my childhood, and early adult life, and it is my prayer that readers see the power of God, and how my nightmares changed, and I began living my dreams. I do hope that by reading this book, you see how Psalms 27 was the guide in my journey.

Chapter One
Who Am I?

I was born September 1, 1964 in Mobile Alabama, the oldest of my mother's three children. My mama told me that she was originally going to name me Jacqueline, but an older family friend suggested "Ilene" as I could somewhat carry on the names of my mother and her mother, who were both named "Irene." I kind of liked the reasoning, but a lot of people forget about the 'L' and just say "Irene" and this is a pet peeve of mine. Nonetheless maybe this was the intention.

My mother was from Mobile as well and she was the 5th child out of six to her parents. My mother was born in a Baptist family and being unwed and pregnant was a shame for her. My mother told me that she was sent away for a while to stay with a maternal aunt in California because of her mother being ashamed to have an unwed pregnant daughter. However, my mom returned to Mobile to give birth to me. My mom also told me that her mother was mean toward her when I was born, even turned off the heat and my mom said she had to warm me with her body at times. I remembered that my mom used to work, and I would stay home with my grandmother, so I do not remember my grandmother being mean. My mom and I lived with my grandmother until I was around 6yrs old. I can remember calling my grandmother mama as well until one day I noticed that when I said "mama" they both answered and then a male cousin and I decided to start calling grandmama 'grandmama'.

At some point my mama married a man named Fred Wright. I don't remember the marriage, but I don't think it lasted long because I do not remember living with him. I do remember him kidnapping my mama one night when me, my mama, and her new boyfriend were leaving the movies. I had to be about four or five. I remember being driven home by my mom's boyfriend, and then I remember the day my mama came home because I was sitting on her lap. I looked back at her, and she had two black eyes after being beaten by her ex-husband. No one ever told me the details about what Fred had done but I imagine his abuse may be why their marriage ended. He may have followed other times as well. Years later I think when I was about 10 years old, Fred stopped me and my little brother when we were walking to the store. He looked at my brother and said "you could have been my son." I do not remember if he said anything to me at all. I don't remember if we made it to the store or not, but I do remember telling my mama about it. She seemed upset about it, but she was not upset with us. I cannot recall a time my mama ever whooped me or said any unkind words to me as a little girl.

I believe my father was born in Demopolis, Alabama, and he was the oldest of three by his mother. He left the Mobile area and moved to Toledo Ohio when I was about three. He and my mother were never married. I later learned that he used to drive trucks before moving to Ohio to work for the Ford Motor Company. My earliest memory of my dad was him dropping me off at my grandma's house from a visit with him. I was about three years old. I don't remember spending any more time with him after he moved away until I was around 12. At that time, he introduced me another female child of his that I was only about four months older than. I can remember hearing her mother say "how did you manage to get two children around the same age in the same town?" He took us to some of his relatives' homes in Hillsdale Height and we took pictures. My sister and I did not talk much that day and did not see each other again until we were around 17 years old. I remember she had a son about that time that was like one-year-old, so she had to have had him at 16. This time my dad was visiting and drove us to Demopolis. We then met his mother and aunt. I later learned that my sister was familiar with the area because that was where her mother grew up and my sister had visited before with her other relatives before I had. My dad had come another time a few years before we were 17 so I was around 14 or so. That time he introduced me to his sons who came with him. One was my age, which he adopted, and the other son was younger. My dad was married by then and had started another family. I did not like the son that was my age as we fought over riding in the front seat. I was hurt when learning about the other children my father had, especially the boys because they got to live with my dad and be around daddy all the time. Another visit my dad made to Alabama was when I was about 15. He always visited in the summertime but this time he did not spend time with me, but with my mother. He tried to speak to me by phone and I did not want to talk to him because I was hurt that he did not visit me in person when I rarely saw him. We did talk sometimes on the phone over the years. The last visit I had from my dad was the summer of 1987 when I finished undergraduate school. He came to my mom's house, but he did not come in, I think because my stepdad was home. My mom was in the backyard hanging clothes on the line and she would not come up front but told me to tell my daddy hello, after he asked me to let her know he was there.

Chapter Two

A Mother's Love

I remember meeting my mom's boyfriend at Christmas when I was four. I recall him talking to me and I was trying to ignore him. I remember having a dollhouse built in my grandma's backyard by her "male friend." I had gotten a Raggedy Ann Doll and table set along with a tea set. Little did I know that my mom's boyfriend would be in my life until I was 32, which was when he died. Me and mom moved in with her boyfriend who later became my little brother and sister's father. We moved in with him when I was about six. The first house was the former house where he had lived with his children and ex-wife. My brother was not born until I was eight. I don't think my mother knew that her boyfriend had more than three boys as I can remember her saying to him that he had lied about actually having four daughters as well.

Our family (including my mom's boyfriend) moved several times and mostly close to my grandma's house.

I must have been getting a little too chubby because I remember being six years old and a doctor placed me on a diet. My mom would cook my food, and hamburgers were my favorite, but she would cook them in the oven. My mother took me off of the diet because she said it looked like my eyes were going back in my head and she could not stand to see her baby looking like that. I remember being part of the desegregation movement and being bused to a predominantly white school several miles from where we lived. My mom decided to ride the bus and work at the school for a while to make sure I was safe. She used to kiss and hug me a lot. I felt she was my best friend and told her about everything that went on in my life. She used to tell me that I could tell her secrets that others told me not to tell, but I would say to her "I gotta tell you mama." My mom's boyfriend was apparently good to her because she stopped working. She cooked for him up to three times a day when he was not working and made sure he had lunch for work. He drove my mama everywhere because she did not know how to drive. In fact, I am the first generation of women in my family to know how to drive. It seemed that he gave her whatever she wanted because they would go off and come back with furniture often.

Chapter Three
The Beginning of Dying

My brother was born when I was 8 in November of 1972. I remember coming home from school to my grandmother's house and there was my little brother. He was the first infant I had ever seen and I remember me and a male cousin asking why my brother could not walk or talk. Life continued to be good. I learned to wash dishes, tie my shoes, and ride a bike without training wheels. My brother was slow to potty train so I can remember changing his diapers for a brief period. He was kind of sickly with asthma often and was even hospitalized for Christmas when he was two and I was 10. That was the year that I learned that Santa Claus was not real because I put out my own gifts that year as I was staying with my grandmother while my mom was at the hospital with my brother.

My mom's boyfriend and I did not interact much at all and this became even more prevalent the older I got, because my mother wanted it that way. I started my period about a month before turning 12 and my mom had just said a few days earlier that I was her baby when she was talking with my grandmother. When my period started my mom said, "Now you are a young lady, my baby is growing up." At the end of that same year in 1976, my mother said she was pregnant. I think that I was excited and hoping for a sister. My sister was born in August of 1977. Summer 1978 my sister was around 9 months old by this time. I began to ask myself, "Am I my sister's keeper?" Apparently, I was and my mama believed that too. I remember my mama telling me, "You better not let my baby fall out of that chair." I replied, "But I want to be able to go outside and play with my friends." My mama reiterated, "I know you better not let my baby fall out of that chair." My sister then falls out of the chair and my mama and I go to get her up. My mom reaches her first saying again, "I told you not to let my baby fall out of the chair." We were both there, but it was my fault and responsibility to make sure that my sister did not fall out of the chair. Well, this was the day I died and my mother said that she did not care if I died. As my sister was crying in my mother's arm, I tried to reach for her, and my mama kept moving so that I could not calm my sister. I felt so bad and for the first time I wanted to die. I reached for pills to take and I heard my brother tell my mama "Ilene fixin to take pills!" My mother replied, "I don't care." That killed me. This was the beginning of my dying.

Chapter Four

Diminishing Me

From that day forward I never complained again about having to take care of my brother and sister. Taking care of them went from summertime to all of the time. The Nightmares Began: I lost my true laughter, and my smiles became fake to hide the pain. After no longer being able to go outside and play, I began to gain weight and food became my comfort. My mother became a bully with constant name calling and planting the seeds that I was nothing and would become nothing. She said that I was going to grow up and be a parasite, a big stand up in the road and my husband would beat me for breakfast, dinner, and supper. She made me feel stupid and less than. When I would try to have friends that were smart, she would say that those smart girls did not want to have anything to do with me, that they did not really care anything about me. She would say that I was fat and not slim and trim as other girls, and they would not want me around. As a matter of fact, she said that she was my best friend. Life was so miserable for me and I felt so all alone.

My mother seemed to become more distant and mean toward me initially after the incident of my sister falling. Right before school began that year, before I turned 13, my mother sent me to get my hair permed.

My mom had complained about being tired of doing my hair because of its thickness and a friend of hers said that she was sending her daughter, who was a classmate of mine, to have her hair permed. So, an older cousin recommended someone at a local hair salon and my mother and her boyfriend dropped me off at the salon one Saturday. I had no idea what a perm was so when my neck started to burn, I did not know what was happening. I was around strange people and was too embarrassed to speak up. I remember the lady saying "oh your neck is burned, why didn't you say something?" The lady put some cream on it but the lye had burned my skin off and my neck was white. It stayed that way for many years. That perm was also the beginning of me having to become responsible for my hair being taken care of. My mother never touched my head to style my hair from that point on, and she would have me ask my friends about who did their hair. I would then go to someone my friends had said did their hair. I guess my mother had decided that either I was old enough to start this or she was not going to be doing two girls' hair. She never discussed it with me and I even started washing and combing my sister's hair. I could only do ponytails and sometimes they would be too tight for my sister and bumps would occur and then my mother would go in on me verbally calling me names like "stupid" and "dumb" or hitting me with her hand because she did not like the way I was doing my sister's hair. I did get a little better and not put the rubber bands on so tight. I would put my hair in ponytails mostly and began to have some hair loss. I did not really know how to take care of my hair. I believe I did not speak up about the burning on my neck out of shyness and fear. I had started to become nervous and concerned all the time about being fussed at by my mother. I was basically a nervous wreck and began to let other people take advantage of me. My self-worth basically became nonexistent.

Chapter Five
No Childhood for Me

My time was divided into me going to school, coming home to take care of my brother and sister, which meant cooking for them sometimes, making sure they did homework, and when they did not want to do it, I would get yelled at because they did not do it. My homework was not important, yet I was expected to get passing grades. If I got bad grades, I would bring shame on the family. I was responsible for making sure my siblings got bathed and put to bed. I also had to make sure their clothes were ready for the next day. I did get to talk to friends on the phone sometimes while I was doing household chores because that was my job as well. I even ironed everyone's clothes except for my stepdad. A couple of times I actually got to go to a couple of football games during my high school years.

I was standing at the bus stop in 8th grade waiting for the bus to pick us up for school. I saw two of my friends kiss each other on the cheeks and called each other best friends. A light went off that this was what I needed in my life. A friend to be my best friend, someone to love me. So, I sought out a best friend. Bessie was the first choice but that did not last long, she would tease me in front of other kids. I tried to buy her friendship and she even said that herself. Lacey, another friend in the neighborhood, and I had attended the same schools for most of our lives. She won the title of queen in our middle school, and I set out to make her my best friend. I tried buying her friendship as well, but Lacey let me know that I did not have to buy her friendship. She tried to make me feel good about myself and I told her all of my troubles at home. She even saw some of the scars (whelps) from the worst beating I remember by an extension cord. As a matter of fact, the beating kind of happened due to my friendship with her. It was Halloween of 1978 and I had asked my friend Lacey to walk to the store with me just to have a chance to be in her presence. When we were walking home, my mama was taking clothes from the line and it began to rain. After saying goodbye to my friend, I went into the house and my mama was in a rage like I never saw before. She said, "You saw me out there getting those clothes in and did not come to help me, but you kept talking to your lord and god! That girl is pretty and smart and don't care about you!" My mom picked up one of our big living room chairs and threw it across the room and I trembled and tried to explain that I was just talking to my friend to tell her to save some candy for my sister during trick or treating because I would be taking my brother and sister trick or treating. I said this so that my mama would see that I was looking out for her children, not myself because I no longer felt like her child but a servant.

My mama made me undress to my bare skin from bottom down. She then told me to lie face down on the bed, and she beat me with an extension cord. I would put my hands behind me to lighten the hits to my behind and she would tell me to move my hand. My siblings and their father said nothing, they just kept watching TV. I still had to take them trick or treating after the beating and was very quiet when going to each house. The next day I wore a long-sleeved shirt to cover the whelps on my arms from the beating the night before.

My friend Lacey and I walked home together that day and she expressed concern about how quiet I had been when I came to their house for trick or treating. I showed her my arms with the whelps and she said "You know people can go to jail for beating their children like that?" I became silent the rest of the way home. We never talked about that situation ever again. I kind of think she might have told her twin sister and possibly their mom, but back then people mostly stayed out of other people's business. My mother was jealous of my friendship with this person because this person even stood up to my mom one day at church. Yes, we went to the same church as well. She told my mother that she should treat me better and my mother said to her "every tree has to bear its own fruit" and my friend responded, "she is your fruit and you should be bearing her." My mother was offended of course and told her that she was just a girl and should not be talking to her like that. Our families knew each other. I shared a friendship with my friend and her twin sister but I was closer to my friend Lacey than her sister. I shared some things with her sister, and I know that my friend shared with her as well. I mean they are twins, so they are each other's best friend. They were considered pretty and smart, and basically they were.

Chapter Six
Will God Let Me Die?

High school had been hard because of the abuse I was experiencing. I didn't have much time to concentrate on my schoolwork because all I wanted to do was to die. Some of the teachers would ask me questions in class and I was scared to respond. Once I had a teacher (Ms. Smith) say, "Look how she jumped when I called her name!" This was the result of my mother terrorizing me. My friend Lacey happened to be in class that day and she told me that she had spoken to Ms. Smith about me, possibly Ms. Smith should not make such comments. This was another reason why that friendship meant so much to me. I will forever be grateful to have had Lacey in my life. I know now that God put her in my life to give me hope and to feel valued.

I think a lot of people may feel scared to answer due to feeling embarrassed if they get the answer wrong. I was in the 9th grade when that incident happened. Lacey also picked me as her secret pal on a project in her Home Economics' class. She would always end her notes with "yo te amos amiga,"in English it means: *I love you friend.* She tried to keep it a secret, but I knew it was her. My grades in the 9th grade had me going to remedial classes in the 10th grade, but my mom put some more fear in me and I brought those grades up because she said, "you ain't doing nothing at that schoolhouse!" During the summer months throughout my high school years I had to work to buy my school clothes for the coming year. I was only able to buy 2 outfits, (2 blouses and 2 pairs of pants). I made this money by selling frozen cups and ice cream cones out of our house for my mama, and I was given a portion of the earnings. I did this so much that I developed calluses on my right hand. I even had to do this during regular school too. She even had me take candy to school to sell. I remember my mama waking me up around 2am on a school night to make an ice cream cone for a classmate that lived across the street from us. Needless to say, I was sleepy during school the next day. I was not really surprised that my momma did that to me but I was upset with my classmate for coming over that time of night.

That summer, in 1980 I was hospitalized after overdosing on pills. I had done this several times but I would always vomit them. When I was put on diet pills, I would play around with them and would throw them up as well. It almost became a game because I did not care about living anymore. I had thrown up in class at summer school one day and was sent home. I told my mama about it and said that I did not want to live anymore. She said, "oh go on somewhere." When she saw me get on my knees, take a pillow and lay my head on it in the rocking chair she called my doctor. The doctor told her to take me to the hospital. They did not have to pump my stomach because I had thrown the pills up. I was admitted for a few days. My mama had an issue because she had planned to go on a church trip to Six Flags over Georgia that weekend with my stepdad. She told me to tell the doctor that she had to go out of town to see a sick friend. The doctor's response to my telling him this was "you are sick too. "My mama voiced that I had ruined her planned trip. My aunt and grandmother had come to visit me in the hospital and brought some gifts with positive statements. My aunt expressed concern and I remember saying to my grandmother that I wanted to die. My grandmother asked why I would want to die, and she mentioned that her boyfriend had died and if he could have lived, he would have wanted to live. I think she told me that God did not want to die yet and believe it or not, I think my mama said the same thing but added that God had something for me to do and He was not going to let me die until I did what He had for me to do. It was odd of her to say anything encouraging to me like this, but I accepted it.

Chapter Seven

Mind On 18

The wisdom my family provided in that moment stuck, along with what Lacey had said at an earlier time:

"When you turn 18 you can leave." I guess I thought that my life would always be the way that it was before she said that, so I became hopeful. However, I really did not have a plan on how to leave at the time.

That was the last time I tried to do anything to harm myself. I became focused on becoming 18 and finding a way to escape. When I got out of the hospital, I called Lacey and told her what I did. She said that my mama had told them that I had been sick. Also, my mama and step daddy dropped me back home and left.

It was business as usual and I was looking after my siblings and selling ice cream all on the day of my discharge from the hospital. About a week later I had to go to see a counselor/psychiatrist at the local mental health center, for follow up after discharging from the hospital.

On the way there, my mama told me not to go in there telling her business particularly about my stepdaddy living with us because she was on welfare and was not supposed to have a man living with us. We were living in Section 8 housing, but I did not know anything about that at the time. My stepdad drove me and the rest of the family to the local mental health center office. My mom went in with me but sat in the waiting room. The first person I met was a lady named Ms. Macadory who said something about me still wearing my wristband from the hospital. She cut it off right then and there. I remember her saying something about I was looking for pity by wearing it. Then I met the doctor or counselor, Evelyn Holt was her name. She was so nice, and besides that the only other thing I remember is her saying is that I would send a bad message to my siblings and they might want to kill themselves one day from my example. That was the only time I got to see Ms. Holt or anyone else until I became an adult. After being hospitalized for overdosing, someone told my mama to talk to me better. I knew someone must have because she taunted me about it one day with my grandmother saying, "You have to be careful how you talk to her, you have to be nice when you talk to her. Yo ass ain't no better than anyone else!"

:: 25 ::

Chapter Eight
Knowing the Father

After my friend Lacey pulled away I began to make some other meaningful friendships, as well as some bullies who pretended to be my friends. I guess these people were more along my speed. They made average grades and were on the less ambitious track that I was on. I held my own in the smartness category in this sect. They never really knew just how bad my life was though. As a matter of fact, my mother seemed to like these friends better. I could hang out with them more, like going to school games. I remember coming home from a football game one night, my mama slammed me against the wall and began choking me with both of her hands. She wanted to know if we had walked home from the game. I was so scared and I could see my stepdad looking over at us and then turning his head back to watch the TV. You see my mom would often make the statement that I was "her's" and no one could tell her how to treat me. She would say "I birthed you; I am the one who carried you for nine months, you're mine." She would even say this to her mother and sister or anyone else that might be around and wanted to comment when she was being mean to me.

Some of my new friends had to care for their younger siblings sometimes too. I think that my mother may have had some deeper issues with my friend Lacey's mother. I still would occasionally see Lacey from time to time. She was the choir director for the youth choir that I got to sing in one time. My mother did not come to church that day, but my aunt, who was my mother's sister came and expressed being proud of me. Yes, me in the church choir. Again, something that was good in my life my mother did not support. I remember her one time asking me to not go to church but stay home with her. Mind you, my little sister and brother, along with their father were home as well. She just did not seem to want me to have something or someone good in my life, to keep me beholden to her. Joining the choir came about from a dream I had. In the dream I was sitting in the back of a small church and Jesus walked up to me and asked me to sing Him a song. I replied that I did not know any songs and Jesus replied "When I come back I want you to sing me a song all the way through." I only got to sing in the choir just one time. *I'm Looking for a Miracle* was the song that I will always remember that we sang that Sunday, so I felt good that I could please Jesus when He returns.

The day I turned 15 I remember my mama giving me my birthday licks. She used a yellow broken broom handle and hit me hard on my thighs, legs, and arms. She did not stop when she reached 15 but added different reasons like one for bad luck, one for good luck, one to grow on and so forth. At 15, I learned about the Holiness religion and lifestyle of inviting Jesus Christ into your life and tarrying for the Holy Ghost to be saved. It was a lot different than what I heard about in the Baptist church my family was a part of. My mama was very critical and made comments about it and even scared my sick grandma by saying that I would be jumping around and maybe hurting myself. I had recently had surgery to remove a cyst from my upper buttocks area and my mama said that going and doing the dancing at that church could make the wound reopen. When she would say that my grandmother would cry out asking me not to do it. After having that cyst, I never had to worry about my mama hitting me back there again. She ensured that the wound from surgery was being cleaned as it was healing.

After having to stop going to the holiness church, I started to watch Oral Roberts on TV some Sunday mornings. I would also write to them and ask different spiritual questions. In the 10th through 12th grade, I pulled my grades up as best as I could. I was not as studious as my special friend Lacey but I had the potential to be an above average student, but there again with all the responsibilities at home and the fear, I did my best. It was very confusing and I even thought I would lose my mind. On another occasion during the summer, I asked my mama about me being able to go outside and not to have to take care of my siblings. She pushed me out and would not let me back in. She said, "You want to go, then stay out!" I began to cry and ask to come back in because it got dark and I was scared. My stepdad and siblings just watched as I begged to get in going from the front door to the back door. My mama told them not to let me in. I went across the street to an elderly neighbor's house that my mama would sometimes visit. Her name was Ms. Davis. She called my mama on the phone and told her to let me back in. She told my mama that I was her child and she needed to let me in. After the call, I was able to get back in the house. Needless to say, I stopped asking to go outside.

Chapter Nine
Not College Material

I went to trade school in the 11th and 12th grade for childcare as recommended by the school counselor. I was not seen as college material apparently by everyone including myself. Even though I was doing what I could with my brother and sister, the childcare class was different. Ms. Nash, a white lady, was our teacher. She was very nice and caring so I had someone in my life that was kind. She never knew about my struggles but I enjoyed the class and the friends I made. One of our classmates died from electrocution over 12th grade Christmas break. Her name was Eve and I had brought her a sandwich for our first day back from the holiday break. I would oftentimes share my sandwiches with her, but that day I brought one for her to have as her own. As we were headed to the bus, someone said, "You heard about what happened to Eve?" I thought nothing as serious as hearing "she died." We were told that the electric heater they used in their bathroom fell in the tub with her. This was so hurtful. Right before we left for the holiday break during the Christmas program Eve sang *Oh Holy Night*. This was the first time I heard that song, Eve had a beautiful voice. My first thoughts when hearing about a child dying was that she must have been disrespectful to her parents. You know the bible says that your days would be long upon land if you obeyed your parents. I was afraid of electricity after Eve's death.

I went to an all-black high school which was where I learned a lot about black history. Something that I had not gotten in my previous years of school. In order to graduate we had to pass both the Math and English parts of what was called a competency exam. I passed both parts on the first try, so I realized that I may not be as dumb and stupid as my mom said I was. Preparing for high school graduation meant getting dresses and shoes to match for all of the girls. In those days every dress had to be the same so everyone had to get someone to make theirs' and my aunt made my dress. Our shoes had to be black but they could be different. My shoes cost $40 and my mom did not want to spend that much on me. She even said that I was not worth spending that kind of money on, but she eventually bought them. It took years before I had another pair of shoes that cost over $40 or anything else for that matter.

In June of 1982 High school graduation happened. My friend Lacey ended up being our high school queen that year and valedictorian. Our friendship had basically fizzled by this time. She did give me a hug and a kiss on the cheek after our Baccalaureate ceremony. Basically, I was not healthy for Lacey. My friend Lacey was very caring and because of my insecurity and wanting to keep her focused on me, I told her a lie that I was dying from a disease. I truly needed this friendship. She also had some health problems with her heart and I think that her mother felt we should not be friends. So you can see that my life was too much for another child to try to intervene, and back in those days adults did not get involved much with how others raised their children. Besides that, my mother's jealousy had her telling me unflattering things about my friend's mother to ensure that I looked negatively upon her. However, it did not work, and I adored their mother for many years. I even talked with her on the phone sometimes after I graduated from college. Of course, my mother really did not know this, and I was living in Montgomery at that time.

That night before going to a graduation party my mama gave me a card and told me that she loved me or either she was proud of me. She even let me go to a graduation party with fellow graduate and friend Patricia that lived in our neighborhood. Just a few months before graduating high school, I sold Avon to some of the students as a way to start some type of job after completing high school. Well, that job fizzled a few days after graduation. My friend Rebecca mentioned that she and a couple of her classmates were going to go to the local Junior College in the fall of 1982. I decided to apply as well. Life continued as usual that summer and I decided to go to Bishop State Community College in the fall. This was good for me educationally because I was put in remedial classes at first. I excelled above most in the classes, and this boosted my self-confidence. There was one teacher there in particular who would point out my accuracy over the other students. However, home life was hell as usual.

Chapter Ten
Bigger Dreams

———————◆———————

In order to start Junior College I needed a $200 loan until my financial aid started. I asked my mom for assistance. She spoke very negatively to me over my request for $200. The same neighbor that told her to let me back in the house when she locked me out, convinced my mother to give me the money. Believe me I was so glad to be able to give that money back to her. I don't believe that my mother believed that I would end up going to college as she had told me that I was a dummy and "Your husband gonna beat you for breakfast, dinner, and supper." During the whole time my mother only gave me $10 a week to ride the bus to Bishop State. On Fridays I would have a couple of dollars left over to eat at a nearby chicken place with some classmates. I made friends with two girls who were actually friends of my friend

Rebecca. One of those girls had a car and occasionally she would pick me up and give me a ride to and from school. They knew that I did not have much money, so they wanted to help me out. Me and these three girls all registered to vote together as soon as we were 8. It felt so good to do this.

I excelled very well while at Bishop State and sometimes my friends would tease me about how the English teacher praised me often. I had planned on majoring in computers because it had a promising future for a good career. I was not pressured to choose a major though, because the low GPA from high school put me in the remedial class level, so I had time to think about what I would major in. At the end of this first year together we all were deciding to go into another direction. My friend Rebecca decided to go to the Navy while me and the other two decided to go to Alabama State University (ASU) in Montgomery, Alabama. I am not sure if we made the decision together or if it was by coincidence. I just remember a girl in the neighborhood named Brenda, who used to relax/perm my hair, mentioned ASU to me in the summer of 1983. She had been attending ASU. I told her that it would be hard for me and I did not have the money and I had never left home before. Well, this girl told me about financial aid paying for basically everything. BOOM! My way out and the resonation of my friend saying, *"when you turn 18 you can leave."*

I had used my grandmother's income to apply for financial aid to have enough to now pay for housing in addition to classes. The guilt soon began to settle in, because I felt that I needed to be there for my siblings and my mother. However, an incident between my mother and my step dad opened my eyes to the fact that he was more important, and she was always going to choose him first. My stepdad apparently was threatening to leave my mama and she had her 22-caliber gun saying if he left, she would shoot herself. This led me to believe that she cared more about him than she did the rest of us, so feeling unneeded there helped push me into leaving. I had developed an aversion to my stepdad basically since I was 10 years old after he hit my mother for talking on the phone to my daddy. There were some other incidents that occurred that affected my feelings toward him, such as a couple of times having to call the police because he threatened to hit my mama. There were also some things I held against him that were not his fault. Rather it was how my mother did not want me to have any contact with him even though he lived with us. I had to always wear a robe in his presence, and he could not touch anything of mine, not even helping assist with carrying things like my luggage when coming and leaving between breaks in college.

Years later I learned why some of this was for my protection. Incest had been an issue in the family and my mother was afraid that the same could happen with me. My initial thinking was, "Why have someone around your children that you don't trust?" But the times dictated that you keep your man around at all costs and to pay your bills. It took years to put this together. Although, my stepdad did not have the opportunity to hurt me, please believe though that the line in the movie *The Color Purple* that says "a girl child ain't safe in a family of men" has a lot of truth to it.

Chapter Eleven

Finally Free

❦

As I was approved for financial aid and accepted to Thee Alabama State University my mother did not like it at all. There were a couple of bullies that pranked me one day before I left for ASU who doubted that I was really going off to college. They pretended to be from the University of Alabama when they called so besides recognizing their voices, having said the wrong school were dead giveaways of their prank. They were laughing and saying, "You know you ain't going to no college!" As mentioned, I was a child in the welfare system so when the social worker came to the house one day, my mom told her about me going off to college. My mother said that she would never write or call if I left. The social worker seemed pleased and said even if I did not get an educational degree, I might get a "Mrs." degree. My mom basically kept her word because she only called me one time during the two years I lived on campus. She did write and send a few dollars from time to time. She never visited either.

My friend Patricia that I mentioned on the night of high school graduation had spent her first year at Grambling State and did not like it. So Patricia decided to try ASU. One of her older sisters had graduated from ASU and she thought that she might like it as well. Needless to say, my mom felt that my going to ASU was Patricia's idea because she had always said that I was a follower and not a leader. It was around 2am on August 18th or 19th,1983, when we arrived at the Greyhound bus station in mobile. My mother had come along and she let me use the same trunk that she had used when she went off to ASU herself, back when it was a teachers college, however, she said that she only stayed less than a year because her asthma was really bad. I don't really remember saying goodbye. However, as I rode that bus my thoughts fell on my little brother and sister, and who would take care of them. I almost turned around to go back once getting to Montgomery. I remember someone saying to me though that I could do more for my siblings by going to get a college education. That they could follow in my footsteps. I had come to love my siblings so very much and was concerned that they would not get the care I had given them.

When Patricia and I stepped off the bus there were several cab drivers vying for us to take them. I think we ended up with

New Deal Cab company. We both were assigned to Abercrombie Hall but not the same rooms or floors. This also had been the same dorm my mom stayed in. I was on the 2nd floor and Patricia was on the 3rd floor. I felt so free as if I was in heaven and never wanted to leave. I purposely made some D's the first semester so that I could stay forever and never have to leave. My thinking was, having to retake those classes because of the low grades would keep me in school longer. However, I quickly learned that this would have some negative consequences on my future.

Chapter Twelve
Welcome to College

I met my roommate at a dance outside on campus. The song Electricity was playing and she was doing the dance called the "snake." I think there was a dance off or something because she was getting down. Patricia said "That is your roommate dancing like that." I asked how she knew and she said she saw her in a picture in my room. My roommate Janice, Jan for short, was from Lower Peach Tree Alabama. I had never heard of it and continued to learn about a lot of places I did not know about in Alabama. Janice had several friends that had come to ASU with her. I did not hang with her much but she and Patricia became friends. For some reason I was eager to kind of be out of my norm and become this free person. I met new people and did not want to associate with others that might have been from Mobile outside of Patricia and the two girls that had gone to Bishop State with me, Justine and Debra.

I indulged with the campus life with enthusiasm. Going to parties, and drinking lots of alcohol to the point of intoxication. I even did pot/weed a couple of times with some new friends. I didn't smoke it directly; it was done through what they called the "shotgun" way. This was like a mouth-to-mouth transaction (lips not touching): The smoker blows out the smoke toward the other person's mouth and that person sucks in, and inhales the smoke. Patricia had asked once why I was behaving this way because it was not my usual. I am not sure what I said to her. All I knew was that I was enjoying myself, hoping it never ended and enjoying my freedom. Drinking alcohol was not new because it was available in my home and back then it was nothing for my mother to allow us, at least me and my brother, to have a beer. I would sometimes sneak the hard stuff when I was older. As a matter of fact, I remember my mom giving me some Morgan David grape wine around age six. It was to help build the blood from what I can remember being told.

I joined the junior club to a sorority that I would later pledge in the following years. I was introduced to the club by some friends in my dorm as they were interested in joining sororities, which was something I never even thought about. Not all the friends I made in the dorm were interested in the same sororities. The advisor Mrs. Casey, to the club I joined, became very nice to me and gave me my first tube of lipstick and later some "Bill Blass" perfume. She also began to ask me to babysit her toddler son, which helped me earn some money. Mrs. Casey was married to a Colonel in the US Airforce and they lived on base. Mrs. Casey would invite me to spend time with her at some personal events such as a cookout at a friend's home. That was the first time I had a grilled steak with a salad. We also went to Denny's when they were here in town. There I had my first silver dollar sized pancakes. Her son was very fond of me and would step to anyone who he thought might cause me any harm. One of the ladies from the sorority was pointing at me one day when she was talking to me and he said "Don't talk to my Ilene like that!" The lady was not being mean to me but he thought so.

My mom and her boyfriend married when I was 18 after I had left to go to Alabama State University. It was a surprise wedding during my Christmas break from school. I was surprised that he was going to church with us because he never went to church, ever, never ever. I remember my mama telling what was to happen when we went to church. She had not told any of her other family until after it was over. I was very sad about them getting married and acted withdrawn at the restaurant we went to after church. My mom told me that my mood was ruining her day. For me it meant that everyone else's last name would change and so I felt more alone. I felt that I was being pushed farther away from being part of their family. For years I had spent most of my time alone in my room and they were a family. Now that my siblings had their father's last name, they were able to move from Medicaid insurance and began using their father's work insurance of Blue Cross and Blue Shield. They were able to get better quality health and dental care. Well with me being 18 now, my benefits with Medicaid had ceased and I could no longer get dental care or continue wearing glasses. When my mom would write letters they would be in her married name and so I would return mail by adding my daddy's last name. My mom asked who's name it was and I told her it was my daddy's and she said that he told her he had a different last name "Lewis". This let me know just how much they did not know about each other.

The first summer after starting at ASU, I went home for the summer break because financial aid did not cover summer sessions, at least I don't think they did. I had work-study which I considered as my first job and according to the government it was. This was when I learned about taxes being taken out of checks. My job was in the cafeteria on the serving line and later moved to the dishwashing area, which I liked better. I mean serving was challenging because you had students complain about various things and plus that meant being front and center around a lot of people at one time. During that summer of 84, my life went back to being the same and I was expected to do the same routine before leaving for college. I was depressed a lot and in fear of having to stay home and not being able to go back to ASU. I was fearing I would not get to experience that joy again.

A new family had moved next door to us. The mother was about 10 years older than me and we became fast friends. Her name was Yasmine and she was overweight like me and she could relate to some of the home issues I was dealing with. Yasmine shared some things about herself that let me know that she could see what I was going through. She was always positive and encouraging to me. Yasmine had a daughter the same age as my brother, a son a few years younger, and a live-in younger boyfriend. Her son had a crush on me and it was cute. As usual my mom did not like me having someone in my life treating me well. Although I had been off to college, my mom wanted me to know that she was still my ruler.

One night while I was visiting Yasmine, my mama locked me out again the same as when I was a teenager. When I knocked on the door, she told me to find somewhere else to sleep. I felt too ashamed to go back to Yasmine's in fear of this making my mom angrier. So I went back over to Ms. Davis's house and she pleaded with my mother to let me back in. My mother said she was upset because I had left the house while she was gone and I did not have her permission to leave the house, although I was just next door. Every chance I got to spend with Yasmine and her family I did, even if it meant taking my little sister along which was most of the time for most things. During breaks from school when I came home,

I would go to Yasmine's house first and then let her drive me home without my mother knowing. This way I was able to have some fun on breaks. However, on one occasion, Yasmine's daughter called my little sister and told her that I was at their house. Needless to say, that turned into a bad time with my mother being mad about it and indicating that I did not appreciate her along with a lack of trust. This only perpetuated her dislike of my friendship with Yasmine.

One day in the summer of 1984 I worked in the field picking peas. I made $20 for the entire long day. This was my planned way to make some money in the summer to give to my mama, and to have some for myself. I caught a truck with some people in the neighborhood to go pick peas in a field. The bag to put the peas in was a large sack called a bushel, I think. The sack got heavier as the day went on and I only picked one bushel for the whole day. I had to drag the bag so dirt got inside of it and the person who was paying said that I had mostly dirt and gave me a $20 bill. Some people had picked several sacks of peas and of course they received more money than me. That work day started out around 6am and we went back home around 5pm. An older lady on the truck that I sat next to said "Baby you need to go back to school. This kind of work is not for you." When I got home from that day in the field, I was so tired and sore. My mama seemed disappointed that I only made $20. She had cooked one of my favorite meals: Big white lima beans and cornbread. I took a hot bath to help relieve my soreness. Needless to say, that lady on that truck was right and I never picked peas again so far.

I went back to selling the ice cream cones and frozen cups as I had done before leaving for college. I was given some of the money to help me get back to ASU for the fall in 1984. I changed work study jobs and moved from the dining hall to the library. I was matched with a supervisor from my hometown area on purpose according to the person doing the assigning.

Chapter Fourteen
A Healing Miracle

In the spring of 1985 at ASU, I began pledging into the youngest African American sorority. I was able to get along with my new found sisters and believed that I would have a new set of family members to count on. However, there was one Soror, Georgia, who always had a dislike toward me. She would pick on me when I was on line as if she was jealous of my relationship with the sorority's advisor and another Soror Victoria, that she had been friends with for many years. Georgia slapped me once while I was on line and she would make fun of me being short and fat. She would say "weebles wobble but they don't fall down" and she even teased me about my low grades.

Victoria had become very special to me. She was kind in a motherly nurturing way toward me and some would call me her baby. Because of her nurturing, I wanted to be around her as much as I could. Victoria allowed me to sleep in the bed with her, mostly at the foot of the bed. Victoria was the mother to a toddler who her parents were taking care of while she was at college. Victoria, Georgia, and Chemika were from the same hometown of Pittsview, Alabama. I had never heard of it. Victoria and Chemika were roommates, prior to the house, and I stayed in their dorm room quite a bit and because Chemika was very kind to me as well, but I was considered special to Victoria and most people knew it, hence Georgia's jealousy.

This same year I declared Psychology as my major with a minor in Social Work. My friend Rebecca had suggested years earlier that I become a psychiatrist because I helped others solve their problems. I had an interest in psychology for personal reasons because I felt that I needed to find out what was wrong with me that would cause my mom to treat me as she did. I also wanted to help people socially as I had benefited from social services myself. As indicated earlier I lost my Medicaid benefits so it was good to have a health clinic on campus to use when I was not feeling well. This did not help with the glasses though and I had worn them since I was six years old.

In the summer of 1985 when I returned home for the summer months my family had moved again. I really believed it was because my mother did not want to be around Yasmine anymore, but that did not stop our friendship. During that summer I was sick with asthma and my mama had me doing my usual of cooking and cleaning. One particular day one of her friends was over and brought some fish. I was charged with cooking the fish for them. We did not have central air and they sat in the room where there was a window air conditioner. I was so hot in that kitchen trying to fry fish and wash dishes. I was wheezing and sweat dripped from my face. I could hardly catch my breath. I went into the bathroom. The floor was covered with a thick carpet and the light was not working, there was a lamp without a shade setting on the floor. The floor was damp and I was barefooted. After I washed my hands, not sure if I dried my hands and I picked up that lamp by the metal part at the top. What happened next was a miracle. An electrical current ran through my hand and I dropped the lamp immediately. However, my lungs cleared and I was able to breathe and felt so much better. (I do not recommend anyone trying this on purpose.)

I did not tell my mama because I knew she would have fussed at me and not really cared about how I was feeling. At least that was her usual response to anything bad happening to me. I was just thankful to be able to breathe better. This was quite a phenomenon and I do not recall having an asthma attack since. I think it just turned into me having severe allergy issues but never anything as serious as an asthma attack.

Chapter Fifteen
Life as an Upperclassman

The next fall at ASU in 1985, Victoria and Chemika had moved into a house near campus. They were renting a 3-bedroom house with one other person named Whitney. Whitney was from another small town that I had never heard of either, Eufaula. Because Victoria and I had been so close, and I was always hanging around them, I moved into Victoria's bedroom and left the dorm. However, when she had a male visitor, I would sleep on the couch. A few months later, since the dining room was empty, I bought a bed and dresser from my work study supervisor, Mary Chames and moved into the dining room area. Ms. Chames later became a second mother to me. Of course, my mama did not like this, but what could she do to me any worse than what she was already doing.

In October 1985, during the fall semester at ASU there was the annual Greek Show. I helped my sorority win the first-place prize in the annual Greek step show. We came out on "Object of my Desire" and the win was when we left off the floor with Dougie Fresh's "6 minutes You're On." We wore blue fedora hats, gold button down shirts, long blue skirts with high heeled shoes. I could not find a gold shirt in my size so I wore a blue sweater. We had surprised our advisor as she thought we were going to wear jeans, but she was pleasantly surprised. I did the dance 'the snake' combined with 'the scooby doo,as the tail dog, last on the floor. I went down on my knees and turned around to face both sides of the audience. The crowd yelled "Ilene, Ilene, Ilene!" I was a star and people stopped me all around campus for days and said, "Girl you did so good!" Some people even now remember me from that night. There was a party that night at our house. Chemika did not know about the party because there had been some misunderstandings in the house and when she came and saw the party, she asked Victoria and the others if they wanted her to move out. I am not sure what their falling out had been about, but I was on the side of Victoria. I really hated that they fell out because I liked Chemika a lot as well. I had even added to the drama by showing Victoria letters I had received from Chemika during the previous summer. I know that this was a bad decision.

Chemika had pledged another sorority and she even congratulated me the night of the step show and party. She did not hang out with us that much because she was very studious and spent a lot of her free time with her boyfriend. We all had fun times together like when I wanted to hang out with them so badly, I had to ride back from a Toga party in the hatchback window of Soror Georgia boyfriend's car. We had gone up to the party at Troy University in Troy, Alabama and visited Victoria's daughter's father and their home girl from Pittsview, Alabama.

Chapter Sixteen
Federal Court

Winter semester of 1986 which begin in January, I was under the impression that I would be moving into Chemika's room since she moved out. To my surprise and disappointment, when I opened the door to what was Chemika's room there was Georgia's things. The sorority trophy in the room along with other paraphernalia was there. I immediately tried to call Victoria and Whitney to see what had happened but could not reach them. Whitney was the second person to return, and she seemed surprised as well. Victoria called trying to disguise her voice and asked to speak to Whitney. I told Whitney to tell Victoria that I said hello. Victoria must have questioned Whitney about how I knew it was her on the phone because Whitney said "She knows your voice." She also said to Victoria, that giving that room to

Georgia was wrong because I had been told that I could move into that room. Needless to say, I was hurt but was told that they needed the extra money because Chemika had left without paying portions of what she owed. The heat was also in Chemika's name, so it was cold when we got back because Chemika had the heat turned off. My hurt led me to move out as Victoria's behavior toward me had changed especially since she started heavily dating this guy, who later became her husband. I did eventually end up apologizing to Chemika especially after the way I was treated by Victoria and Georgia.

Sometime prior to moving out from Victoria and the rest, I almost spent time in federal prison. Although Georgia had treated me the way she had, I made an effort to try to support my sorority sister by going with her to Maxwell Air Force base to wash her clothes. I did not know about trespassing and did not think that was what we were doing because Victoria's boyfriend was in the military and Victoria had a pass to get on base. If I had known that we were not to be using the laundry facility I would not have been walking outside studying for my Spanish test. Well, the Military Police (MP's) came with dogs and made us leave in the middle of Georgia washing her clothes. She blamed me for being outside, but she had not been honest with me about it not being ok for us to be there. Months later, after moving out from Victoria and Georgia, Justine (who also pledged with me) told me that while she was visiting with Georgia and Victoria, a deputy came to their house to serve us for court. Well according to Justine, Georgia and the others decided not to tell me about the notice. At that point I decided to talk with Mrs. Casey about what happened. She asked why had I not told her about the incident when it happened as she could have stopped the charges due to her husband's military rank. Mrs. Casey made a phone call, and I was given a chance to have another hearing because I missed the first hearing, and therefore in contempt of court. I had to go to the federal court building and I was terrified when I got there. I had to take the city line bus and I missed part of work study that day. When the judge asked me to give him a reason why he should not sentence me to 6 months in jail, I looked over at the two attorneys that were to be to help me, they both looked away. I responded to the judge and said, "Because I did not know what I was doing." He fined me 50.00, $25 for trespassing and $25 for being in contempt for missing the first hearing. I had originally asked to break the fine into two payments but when I got to the window to pay, I paid the fine in full because I wanted to get it over with. This had been the last straw with Victoria and Georgia.

This incident was another example of me realizing that I had become involved with people who really did not care about me. I ended up moving in with some other friends that used to work with me when I worked in the cafeteria. The names of my two new housemates were Annie and Annie both of their middle names began with a 'B' and all three of our last names began with 'H.' These two became my best friends throughout the rest of my life. Living with them was much easier, except one of the Annie's was a little stingy at times. We all graduated that same year as well. I felt more independent and no pressure to act like I was inferior to anyone.

Chapter Seventeen
Friend or Foe

Around this time I met Evelyn, and we became friends. She would ask me about how much I had cared for Victoria and what would I do if Victoria died? Well, that was a loaded question. Evelyn was about 10 years older than me. She was married and pregnant with a little girl already. Evelyn instantly became like a mother figure and I would say to her that she sounded like a mom. She was an undergrad student at ASU as well. She was in a couple of my social work classes and also in the library for work study. Evelyn was quite spiritual and I learned more about faith from her. She was also very brash in her speech. I spent time with her and her family, immediate and extended. I began to go to church with her and was supposedly the godmother to her son once he was born. She had always questioned why I was so attached to her and said that I was needy. Evelyn told me once that I was like the woman at the well in the bible, looking for love in all the wrong places. She was probably the first person since my childhood friend that I shared about how my home life was. Evelyn had even traveled to Mobile with me once to meet my mama to get a spiritual feel on things. She concluded some family curses that needed to be broken. I began to move on everything Evelyn would say. I mean she was saved and had the calling of an intercessory prayer. She prayed often.

When her brother moved here from Texas with his wife and son, I joined his church with Evelyn. Her brother had studied under Pastor John Osteen in Texas, The Rhema Word. Here again my faith and knowledge of Jesus was building. I even got baptized again because I was told that I needed to be baptized in the name of Jesus. I had previously been baptized in the name of The Father, The Son and The Holy Ghost. However, because of my issues when Evelyn said that I was bad, I believed it. Not realizing that she had some issues of her own. She had a lot of influence over most of the people in the church. Others in the church would stop talking to me if she was not talking to me. Some years later, during one of Evelyn's times of paranoia she said to me, "You are an uncircumcised Philistine and you came to kill, steal, and destroy." Wow, right? Evelyn had questioned why I wanted to be her friend. Her brother stated once that when he met me and saw that Evelyn and I were friends, he said that I must be hard up for friends. I'm guessing low self-esteem was an issue for her as well. However, she seemed to indicate once that I was attracted to her for homosexual reasons, which was totally not true. Of course, I did eventually stop going to that church and accepted that something was not quite right with Evelyn.

Chapter Eighteen
Graduation, A Job, and a Car

In April of 1987 I started working at St Margaret's Hospital as a patient transporter. A friend of mine named Darlene from my work study job told me about the job. She also would also take me to work sometimes or I would ride the bus. I had gotten my driver's license on December 30th, 1986. I had asked God to allow me to get my license before that year was over and He had a sense of humor of letting it be the last day of the year that the license office would be open. I had been getting in some driving from time to time. I was the first woman in my family to get a driver's license or drive themselves during that time. I was not completely confident in driving because I rarely had times to practice driving, Evelyn teased me about having to wait on the bus. From those comments I became angry and hurt because she said it in front of whoever the person that was with her. This helped me to channel my energy into using a promotion from Chevrolet providing $500 down payment to college graduates that year. I was nervous about driving and when I bought the car someone was to drive it for me. However, that person showed up in their own car and said I would have to drive on my own. I was so scared because I had to drive it on the interstate and I had not driven on the interstate but maybe once in my practicing. I bought a silver 1987 Chevrolet Spectrum. My two housemates also decided to use the same deal and bought the exact same car as I did. However, they did not have driver's licenses and took driver's lessons.

In June of 1987 I graduated from Thee Alabama State University with a Bachelor's of Science in Psychology with a Minor in Social Work. I received a call from my daddy that day to congratulate me and to tell me that earlier in January of that year, he fathered twin girls. He later sent me pictures of them. My mama had come with my stepdad driving. I don't remember my brother and sister being there but I believe they were. I did not get to spend time with them after the graduation, but they did trail me and my roommates to the civic center downtown Montgomery. At that time this was where ASU and other local colleges held their graduations. This was the first time my family had ever traveled to see me. My stepdad was anxious to be off the road before dark. I remember after graduation meeting them at my step dad's car and giving my diploma to my mama. She seemed very proud and touched. She said something about how our names are similarly spelled, her name Irene and mine Ilene. She was tearful and somewhat disappointed that I would not be coming back home because I wanted to continue working at my part-time job at St Margaret, with hopes of getting a job at the local mental health center. I had some trouble at work at one point where I became afraid that I was going to lose my job. To me losing that job would mean that I would have to move back home and all of the goodness that I had experienced would be over. As if I had been living in a dream. I can remember calling Evelyn to tell her about being scared about having to move back home and she said, "You won't have to go back home." This fear haunted me for years.

Through this journey of becoming a now college educated young lady, I discovered I might not be a bad person, but there were times where I allowed myself to be mistreated and placed in unhealthy situations, but yet I was growing. I learned how to survive and thrive, and as already stated God placed the people in my path to lead and guide me. I remember having to come home for holidays and like I said, my family never came to visit me. People would offer rides for $10 and when I did desire to go home, I would accept those offers. On one of the road trips back to Montgomery during my first year at ASU, the car almost caught fire and there was a lot of smoke and we had to pull over. Everyone had to get their bags from the trunk. We drove back very slowly and did not get back until very late after midnight.

When I walked into my room, Janice asked what happened and I fell on my knees and started thanking God that we made it back safe. Janice started laughing and ran upstairs to get Patricia and I told them what happened. They said that they had been concerned.

During the holidays I would mostly ride the bus again because I would have more stuff to take home because the dorms were closing for the holiday break. I used to be so afraid that I would get trapped at home so I used to look forward to getting back to ASU because it was my safe haven. As I mentioned earlier, I wanted to stay as long as I could but when those grades started to look bad and my mama said "you ain't doin nothing at that school house, you can come back home" needless to say, I kept those grades up and even began to think about never returning permanently to Mobile. When I rode the bus I used to love to hear the bus driver say "Montgomery, Montgomery " and until this very day whenever I come back from a trip to Mobile, I say "Montgomery, Montgomery," sometimes aloud even if someone is riding with me or in my head all the time.

When I left home it was obvious that my siblings were being neglected. They didn't have to do homework or clean the house. They were basically doing what they wanted. I did have a little lead way to discipline them by whipping them. I mean this was all I knew, and I would use a belt. I don't think I hurt them the way I was hurt. There were times when I used a belt on them and it would turn on me, and my mama would get into my face and say "have your own children and whoop them." This was one of those situations where I would get confused because I never knew what mood my mom would have toward me from day to day. Even some nice moments like my birthday when I was 15 could turn into a fearful moment. I know that my siblings did not like that I would come home and tell them what to do, especially my brother because he would say that he hated it when I came home. However, there would be times that our mama would say "I told them you were coming home and you would tell them what they need to be doing." My brother even said a couple of times that he wished that I would get into an accident going back to Montgomery. My mama would later tell him not to say such things.

My mom and stepfather opened a little grocery store and they worked there a lot. They would get my sister from school and have her there at the store with them. My brother said once when I went home "Ilene, mama is never at home." I saw it for myself on some visits. My mama and stepdad would come home late around 11pm or later and get up early the next day to go to the store. My brother ended up dropping out of school when he was almost 16. I called the board of education to see what could be done to make him stay in school. The person at the board applauded me as his sister, trying to make him stay in school. They said that they would follow up with him but once my brother turned 16 there was nothing to be done to keep him in school. My brother ended up dropping out of school permanently.

At a certain point, I did have to realize that as an adult with a college degree, there were many doors that could open for me. The Almighty God most certainly had His hands on my life, and I would be nowhere without Him. My story continues and there is still more to be told, but in this one, I want to leave you with knowing that prayer and perseverance, along with faith will impact your life's journey positively. "Trust in the Lord with all thine heart; and lean not unto your own understanding. In all your ways acknowledge him, and He will direct your path." ~Proverbs 3:5-6

The End

Contact the Author

Email: ilene236117@gmail.con

Facebook: Ileene Holcombe

Suicide and Crises Hotlines

Suicide

Call or Text: 988

Crises

Call or Text: 741741